City of Chester

The ancient City of Chester, on the banks of the River Dee, is as much a delight to the visitor today as it was two centuries ago. This thriving centre of commerce and administration has not forgotten its nineteen hundred years of history. Within its medieval walls, buildings of every age are to be found, carefully and lovingly restored and providing a colourful backdrop to life in its busy streets.

Nor will you want for entertainment. Flat-racing on England's oldest race-track, regattas, theatre and music festivals are just a few of the diversions which Chester has to offer.

Stroll through Chester at your leisure and take home memories of the black-and-white buildings, the unique covered walkways of the Rows, and the peace of the cathedral and the riverside walks.

I behold the ground-work of buildings in the streets, laid with main strong huge stones, it seemeth that it hath been founded by the painful labour of Romans, or giants . . .

RANULF HIGDEN, 14TH CENTURY

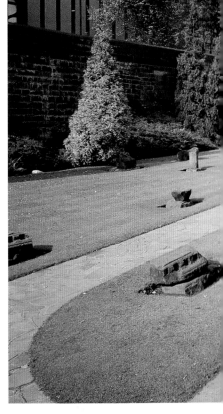

ABOVE: *The hypocaust was the basis of the Roman central heating system. Heated gases were carried by convection from a furnace, under the floor and into the walls of the building. This example was discovered beneath a restaurant in Bridge Street.*

RIGHT: *Amid the fine collection of tomb-stones, altars and inscriptions in the Grosvenor Museum is this memorial to Caecilius Avitus from Merida, Spain, who died at the age of 34 while serving in the XX Legion.*

PRECEDING PAGE: *The 14th-century Old Dee Bridge.*

P resent-day Chester stands on the site of an ancient Roman fortress, built in about AD 79 as a base for military operations against the Welsh. The fortress was constructed on a sandstone plateau in a bend of the River Dee (hence 'Deva') where the river formed a natural moat on two sides. This was the lowest point of the river at which a bridge could be built and the highest point to which sea-going craft could navigate.

The original fortress, of turf and tim-ber, was eventually replaced with stone, and with brick and tiles made at a factory at Holt. Roman stone-cutting techniques were superior to those of medieval masons and much has survived the centuries and can be seen at scattered sites around the city and in the collections at the Grosvenor Museum.

The High Cross, for centuries the centre of activity, stands at the intersection of the old Roman streets: the Via Principalis (now Eastgate and Watergate Streets) run-ning from east to west, and the Via

LEFT: *The Roman Garden, just outside the Newgate, was laid out in 1949 and houses some of the many Roman remains which have been excavated in the city. The columns are from the legionary baths and, in the foreground, is a reconstruction of a hypocaust.*

Decumana (now Northgate Street) and the Via Praetoria (now Bridge Street) running from north to south. These streets linked the four main gates and near their intersection stood the headquarters of the military government and the commandant. Excavations elsewhere in the city have revealed evidence of bath-houses, granaries, barracks and temples.

The fortress was first occupied by the 2nd Adiutrux Legion and then by Agricola's XX Valeria Victrix Legion. Later it became a 'citizen fortress' rather than a centre of active campaigning. The Romans relied on local produce and materials – salt from Cheshire, minerals from North Wales and Anglesey – so Chester undoubtedly became a trading centre. Coal was unloaded at Heronside – the first recorded instance of the Romans using coal.

LEFT: *The northern half of the amphitheatre, which lies to the southeast of the walls, was excavated in 1929–34 and again in 1965–69. Possibly the largest in Britain (it could accommodate 7,000 people), it was used for military exercises, gladiator and beast shows, and, to a lesser extent, for executions. In the foreground are the remains of a shrine to the goddess Nemesis, which lies to the west of the north entrance. The Chester Visitor Centre can be seen in the distance.*

The Romans withdrew in AD 383 and little is known of this 'fortress of the legions' for several centuries. It was probably never completely deserted and the first Saxons are believed to have settled there in AD 650. King Aethelred of Mercia is credited with founding two churches: St John, outside the walls, and St Peter and St Paul, on the site of the present cathedral. King Egbert is recorded as taking Chester in AD 829 and his son Aethelwulf as being crowned there ten years later. It would thus appear that the Saxons were firmly established in the city by this time, although scarcely anything remains of their wattle, clay and timber buildings.

At the beginning of the 10th century, the Norse-Irish community, which had been given land by Aethelred, Aeldorman of Cheshire, allied with the Danes in an unsuccessful attack on Chester. His wife, Aethelflaeda (the 'Lady of the Mercians'), restored the fortress, rebuilding and extending the walls, and raised a castle near the river, outside the former Roman defences. (Chester was one of many towns

or 'burhs' which were fortified at this time.) She also re-dedicated the Church of St Peter and St Paul to St Werburgh and dedicated a chapel to St Oswald and a church to St Peter.

The port of Chester flourished. A Norse-Irish community, probably involved with the tanning and processing of hides, established itself in Lower Bridge Street and a thriving mint developed. Chester thus began to regain its former status, a fact possibly recognised by the Saxon King Edgar reputedly being rowed in state from his palace to St John's Church by eight Celtic kings who had come to swear allegiance to him.

ABOVE: *The Roodee probably dates from the 5th or 6th centuries and stands on the site of the old Roman harbour. Its name comes from the Anglo-Saxon rood meaning 'cross' and ee, 'an island'. Today, it is one of the oldest racecourses in the country.*

ABOVE LEFT: *This silver penny was made by Moneyer Othulf and came from the Chester mint of Aethelred II.*

OPPOSITE: *The relics of St Werburgh were brought to Chester from Hanbury in Staffordshire in the early 10th century for safe-keeping. Her shrine now lies in the lady chapel of the cathedral. Built c. 1310, it has been partly restored.*

OPPOSITE: *The magnificently carved choir stalls are early 14th-century work.*

ABOVE LEFT: *The cloisters have been largely rebuilt and restored.*

ABOVE RIGHT: *The great west window in*

the nave is the recent (1961) work of W. T. Carter-Shapland.

BELOW: *This splendid pelican is carved on the arm of the Vice-Dean's stall.*

The present cathedral stands on the site of the Anglo-Saxon church of St Werburgh, where Hugh d'Avranches, aided by Bishop Anselm, founded a great Benedictine Abbey in 1092. The Abbey flourished as a centre of monastic life, attracting many pilgrims, until the Dissolution of the Monasteries in 1540. A year later, the Abbey Church became the cathedral of the newly formed diocese of Chester. Although the cathedral is still essentially medieval, most of the original building has been replaced over the centuries.

The oldest parts of the cathedral, dating from the 12th century, are to be found in the north transept and in the cloisters. Leading off the cloisters is the 13th-century refectory containing a beautiful stone wall-pulpit and a fine arch-braced hammerbeam roof by F. H. Crossley (1939). Also dating from the 13th century is the chapter house, with its ancient cupboard made in the reign of Edward I, and the lady chapel containing St Werburgh's shrine.

In the 14th century, the monks extended the south transept and work was begun on the nave. Beside the west window, the Norman arches open into the baptistry and a door leads to the uncompleted southwest tower (begun *c.* 1580) which houses the 17th-century consistory court. Above is a fine timbered ceiling dating from the 16th century.

Extensive restorations were carried out in the latter part of the 19th century. The organ loft, choir screen and many of the stained glass windows are of this period, as are the flying buttresses and battlemented parapets, and the south face of the south porch, designed by Sir George Gilbert Scott and Thomas Harrison respectively.

... this region, in fertility of soile commeth behind many Countries in England, yet it hath alwaies bred and reared more Gentry than the rest.

WILLIAM CAMDEN, *BRITAIN*, 1610
(PHILEMON HOLLAND'S TRANSLATION)

In 1070, four years after the Battle of Hastings, Chester was captured by William of Normandy. The earldom of Chester was created the following year and thus the city passed into the hands of a succession of eight Norman earls, the last of whom died in 1237, at which time the earldom of Chester reverted to the Crown. Under the harsh rule of the Normans, Chester became a virtually independent kingdom with its own laws, taxes, nobility, army and courts of justice.

Despite the destruction of many buildings by fire, and the sweeping away of the bridge by floods in 1227, the traditional industries continued. Chester became the principal port for the northwest of England and, in 1175, received its first royal charter confirming trading rights with Ireland. The next two centuries were to see Chester's most prosperous period as a port. Raw materials – hides, cloth and Irish linen and wool – were imported, together with

ABOVE LEFT: *The Falcon Inn at the top of Lower Bridge Street dates from the 14th century.*

LEFT: *King Charles's Tower, at the north-east angle of the Roman fortress, is the most complete of the medieval towers in Chester.*

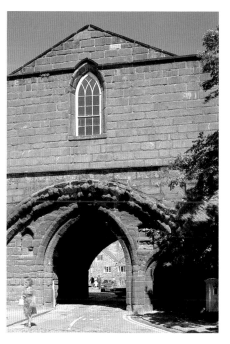

luxury items such as French wines, Spanish ironware, fruits, and spices, and local products such as cheese, salt, gloves and candles were exported.

Chester was again used as a base for campaigns against the Welsh but, after the defeat of Llywelyn ap Gruffydd by Edward I, it began to enjoy a greater measure of security. In 1300, Edward I granted Chester to its citizens in return for a 'fee farm rent' of £100 a year and this did much to encourage the development of the system of self-government, which is still a feature of Chester today.

ABOVE: *St John's Church is a fine Norman building, standing on the site of an Anglo-Saxon church. It was once the cathedral of the diocese of Lichfield.*

LEFT: *The powerful Abbey Gateway is of 14th-century origin. The upper storey was rebuilt in the late 18th/early 19th century.*

*. . . a man may go dry . . . in Galleries,
which they call,* the Roes, *which have
Shopps on both sydes, and underneath with
dyvvers fair staires, to go up or down into
the street.*

ANON, 16TH CENTURY

ABOVE: *The Tudor
House at Numbers
29 and 30 Lower
Bridge Street is
reputed to be the
oldest house in
Chester and dates
from c.1503. It has
been beautifully
restored in recent
years.*

LEFT: *Stanley Palace,
in Watergate Street,
was built by Peter
Warburton, a lawyer
and MP for Cheshire,
and dates from 1591.
It became the town
house of the Stanley
family of Alderley
and later passed to
their kinsmen, the
earls of Derby, who
controlled the tolls
on the nearby
Watergate. It was
leased to the City
Council in 1928 and
has since been
extensively restored.*

RIGHT: *Foregate
Street lies beyond the
Eastgate, on the
route of the old
Roman Watling
Street. A cluster of
buildings grew up
around the street.
Number 70 is one of
the few surviving
Tudor houses and
dates from 1571.*

In Tudor times, life, like the shops and houses, was centred along the four main streets of Chester but fields and orchards were still to be found within the walls. Many medieval buildings, including the cathedral and castle, were altered or rebuilt and many timber buildings were destroyed in the fire of 1565.

The silting of the Dee meant that larger vessels were forced to anchor some 10 miles downstream at Neston but smaller boats could still moor at the Water Tower. Industry flourished and the craft guilds, which looked after the interests of their members by regulating prices, wages and trading, became increasingly powerful. In 1506, Henry VII recognised the Assembly as the city's governing body and Chester's independence of the rest of Cheshire.

Life was busy and prosperous, with lavish entertainments and public spectacles, regular markets, two annual fairs and the spectacular Midsummer Show. The annual Shrove Tuesday football match, which began on the Roodee, was banned in 1539–40 'by reson of the greate hurte and strife' but was replaced by archery contests and by foot- and horse-races.

The Mystery Plays were an essential part of the city's pageantry. The guilds had been involved in their production since 1422, when a play was first performed for

LEFT: *The Pied Bull in Northgate Street is one of Chester's oldest inns. It was the residence of the Recorder in 1553 and, for the most part, dates from this century. In 1664, it was rebuilt in brick and the frontage over the pavement was added in the 18th-century. A coaching inn since 1780, it bears a sign giving the distances between Chester and London and various other destinations.*

the festival of Corpus Christi. By the 16th century, a complete cycle of 25 plays was being presented over the three days of Whitsuntide. Mounted on a wheeled 'pageant-wagon', each play was performed first at the Abbey Gateway and then at the High Cross. Thereafter, the wagons were drawn to a number of stations around Chester where each play was performed in turn. The plays, banned in 1575, were revived by Chester City Council in 1951.

ABOVE: *The Mystery Plays were based on the Bible stories and allocated appropriately among the companies in the city. Thus the Water-drawers of the Dee would enact the story of the Flood and the Bakers would stage the Last Supper.*

The Civil War, which began in 1642, affected Chester profoundly. The Royalists in the Assembly greatly outnumbered the Puritans and Chester declared its support for King Charles I. Troops were stationed at Chester and the defences were prepared. Thus, from 1644 until its surrender to the Parliamentarians in 1646, Chester was besieged. Many buildings were destroyed and a heavy burden was placed on the city treasury which was expected not only to support the siege but also to subsidise the Royalist cause. One hundred pounds' worth of silver civic plate was melted down for coinage. Charles I visited Chester twice during the war, once in 1642 and again in 1645, when he is reputed to have watched the defeat of his army at Rowton Moor from the city walls.

By the end of the 17th century, Chester had recovered its fortunes and was developing into a wholesale and retail regional marketing centre. It had a thriving coastal trade as well as trade with the Mediterranean, Baltic and North America. Neston

LEFT: *The Nine Houses in Park Street (although they now number only six) are a row of timber-framed almshouses, built on a sandstone base, an unusual combination of materials for Chester. They are dated 1658.*

FAR LEFT, BELOW: *The Bear and Billet (1664), just inside the Bridgegate, was the town house of the earls of Shrewsbury until the mid-19th century. The two rows of windows contain over 1,000 panes of glass.*

LEFT: *The right-hand gable of Bishop Lloyd's House in Watergate Street has some extraordinarily fine carving on the exterior panels.*

BELOW: *The frontage bears a series of richly coloured panels depicting a variety of heraldic beasts, biblical scenes, the Legs of Man and the Arms of James I.*

declined as a port and was superseded by Parkgate both for trade and as an embarkation point for passengers. The manufacture of snuff and tobacco, pipes and felt hats was introduced, and shipyards and a temporary royal mint were established.

There was expansion of existing buildings, new housing and new public and commercial buildings. Timber remained the most important building material until the late 17th century. With the introduction of brick, many of the half-timbered houses were refaced and, because of the fire risk, all thatched roofs were replaced with either tile or brick. Thus began the transformation of Chester.

LEFT: *God's Providence House (1652), in Watergate Street, was the only house to be untouched by the plague in the 17th century. In the 1860s, plans to demolish the building provoked such a public outcry that it was restored in 1862 to its original style, using some of the original timbers. At the same time, the windows were enlarged and the decorative plasterwork, or pargetting, was added.*

CENTRE LEFT: *The abbey cottages date from 1626 and are built of sandstone. They stand on the site of the abbey kitchens.*

OVERLEAF: *The Bridge Street Rows.*

I was quite enchanted at Chester, so that I could with difficulty quit it.

BOSWELL, 1779 (LETTERS TO DR JOHNSON)

BELOW: *From the waterside promenade of the Groves, shaded by trees, one can still take a pleasureboat along the river or sit in the*

The 18th century, and the establishment of the turnpike trusts, brought a great improvement to the road systems throughout the country. Chester became a centre for coaching and carrying and its charm and distinction began to attract such increasing numbers of visitors that, at one time, there were no less than 140 licensed inns and taverns in the city.

Chester adapted to this new role: new public and commercial buildings were erected, fashionable villas were built and formal 'London-style' terraced housing was introduced, such as that on the north and west sides of the Abbey Square.

Whole stretches of the Rows, the unique galleried walkways above the shops, disappeared as they were enclosed by their owners but those which remained

sunshine and enjoy a
concert in the
delightful Edwardian
bandstand.

LEFT: *Chester Castle
was begun in the
time of William the
Conqueror but was
rebuilt between 1788
and 1822, in
Classical style,
by the architect
Thomas Harrison.*

BELOW: *The Bishop's
House, on the corner
of Abbey Street and
Abbey Square, is a
fine example of
18th-century archi-
tecture. It was built
by the Chester
builder Edward
Spencer.*

BELOW, LEFT: *This
view c.1780 shows
Chester Castle before
its Classical
transformation by
Harrison, and the
Old Dee Bridge.
The churches of St
Mary's-on-the-Hill
and St John can also
be seen.*

LEFT: *The Grosvenor Bridge was designed by Thomas Harrison and opened by Princess Victoria in 1832. It was the longest single-span bridge in the world at the time.*

BELOW: *On the north and west sides of Abbey Square there are some splendid Georgian terraces displaying fine attention to detail.*

OPPOSITE: *This Georgian scene shows part of the west side of Northgate Street.*

BELOW, RIGHT: *The present Eastgate, which replaced the medieval gate, was built in 1768–69.*

were improved and many high-class shops became established beneath their protective canopies. The four medieval gateways were replaced with ornamental arches, completing the restoration of the walls and providing a walkway around the city. In 1732 the Groves, along the riverside, were created a public walkway and, in 1817, a new grandstand was opened on the Roodee to house the ardent race-goers.

The city was fortunate to escape the worst ravages of the Industrial Revolution and the only factories to become established were a lead-shot works and an hydraulic engineering works. Despite slow progress in the canalisation of the Dee, Chester finally became linked into the national canal network towards the end of the 18th century and became part of the Shropshire Union System.

Chester became a popular resort with landed families, who were attracted by the fashionable entertainments offered by the assembly rooms at the Exchange, Booth Mansion and the Royal Hotel. There were concerts, balls, lectures and plays and, for the more active, cock-fighting, bowling, boating, taking the air and, the highlights of the season, the races and the Assizes.

Chester continued to prosper in Victorian times. Many commercial establishments were built in the centre and many of the older buildings were reconstructed. Medieval revival was the fashion and the city's characteristic black-and-white appearance was created largely by such architects as John Douglas and Thomas Meakin Lockwood. Other styles are also evident. The National Westminster Bank, for example, on the corner of Eastgate Street and St Werburgh Street, was built in a classical style by George Williams in 1859–60, and the Dutch or Flemish style of the Midland Bank, near Eastgate, is another design by John Douglas.

The railway links from Chester to Crewe and to Birkenhead were opened in 1840. City Road, linking the General Railway Station and Foregate Street, together with Grosvenor Road, which linked the recently opened Grosvenor Bridge with Bridge Street, were the first major changes

to the medieval street pattern.

In 1852, the suspension bridge across the Dee was opened and shortly afterwards plans were laid for the suburb of Queen's Park. The poorer districts of the city were gradually improved: water closets were introduced in 1878 and terraced housing was built for skilled workers. An impressive amount of restoration and reconstruction of the cathedral and other public buildings was also carried out during this period, but Chester retained its unique character and continued to flourish.

ABOVE: *The General Railway Station, designed by C.H. Wild and Francis Thompson, was built by Thomas Brassey and completed in 1848.*

LEFT: *The elegant Queen's Park Bridge was first built in 1852 to link Chester with the suburbs of Queen's Park.*

FAR LEFT: *Chester Town Hall was opened in 1869 by HRH The Prince of Wales. It replaced the late 17th-century Exchange, which was burned down in 1862. Designed by William Henry Lynn, it has a central tower rising to 160 feet (48 m). The clock commemorates Chester's 1900th anniversary.*

RIGHT: *The Eastgate Clock was erected in 1899 to commemorate the Diamond Jubilee of Queen Victoria.*

LEFT: *The Eastgate Rows overlook the bustling streets below. The Boot Inn (right) is one of Chester's oldest taverns.*

ABOVE: *The Cross, for centuries a centre of government and trading, was restored to its original position in the mid 1970s. The office of Town Crier was also resurrected and proclamations are now issued regularly from April until September.*

Chester today has escaped the large industrial developments in neighbouring areas to become a thriving hub of local government, administration and commerce, as well as a centre for visitors. The atmosphere and charm of the city and the easy access to the beauty spots of Cheshire, North Wales and Merseyside make it an ideal base for touring.

Chester is quite remarkable for its architectural innovation and for the care which has been lavished on restoring its historic buildings. It was the first British city to appoint a conservation officer and, in 1975, the Chester Heritage Centre – the first Architectural Heritage Centre in Britain – was opened. As a result of its extensive programme of renovation, Chester won the 1982 European Prize for the Preservation of Historic Buildings. The prestigious Europa Nostra Medal was won for the second time in 1990.

The size of the city is such that its treasures, which are all carefully signposted, can be experienced easily on foot. There are regular guided tours – you can even walk around the walls with a Roman soldier! – and excellent information centres. The Rows, which conceal a modern shopping precinct, offer a tantalising variety of shops, taverns and eating-houses, where you can stroll unhindered by the traffic or the elements.

In 1979, Chester celebrated its 1900th anniversary and, in recognition of its 500 years of independence from the county, Queen Elizabeth II granted the city two charters, allowing it to retain many of the ancient privileges confirmed in the Great Charter of 1506. Thus, as Chester enters its twentieth century, the Mayor of the city is still permitted to have his sword carried before him with the point upright and still retains the title 'Admiral of the Dee'.

BELOW, LEFT: *Clusters of narrowboats can be seen around Northgate Lock, near the Water Tower.*

RIGHT: *St Michael's Buildings, in Bridge Street, were completed in 1910.*

BELOW, RIGHT: *The impressive entrance to St Michael's Buildings leads into this cool, lofty arcade and thence into a modern shopping precinct.*

The Cheshire Military Museum
The Castle
The history of local regiments is shown in a fascinating series of displays, housed in the northern block of the Castle.

Chester Heritage Centre
Bridge Street
This offers information on Chester's conservation programme by means of audio-visual presentations and temporary and permanent exhibitions on the history, archaeology and architecture.

Chester Visitor Centre
Vicar's Lane
This offers a video-presentation of Chester's history, an electronic map showing the development of Chester and a life-sized reconstruction of a street in the 1890s. Information, details of accommodation and other facilities for the visitor are available.

Grosvenor Museum
Grosvenor Street
The history and construction of the Roman fortress is displayed in detail, together with a fine collection of Roman gravestones and altars. The museum is also noted for its collection of local watercolours, natural history and archaeology.

Castle Street Period House
20 Castle Street (part of Grosvenor Museum)
This restored 17th-century building leads off from the museum and houses a series of rooms depicting life in a town house from the late 17th century until Victorian times.

St Mary's Centre
St Mary's Hill, off Castle Street
This beautifully restored 15th-century church is now a lively educational and cultural centre.

ABOVE: *This reconstruction of a Victorian schoolroom is in the Castle Street Period House.*

ABOVE, CENTRE: *St Michael's Church was re-opened in 1975 as the Chester Heritage Centre, to celebrate Chester's achievements in conservation.*

ABOVE, FAR RIGHT: *A German clockwork carousel, c. 1905, from the Chester Toy and Doll Museum.*

RIGHT: *The Newstead Gallery of the Grosvenor Museum houses a fine collection of Roman material.*

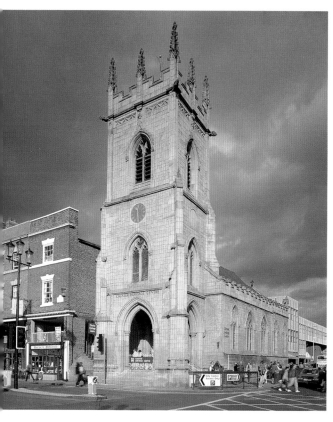

The Toy and Doll Museum
13a Lower Bridge Street
More than 1,000 toys – Victorian and
china dolls, dolls' houses and teddies to
1920s, pedal cars and German, French and
English tinplate toys. Large exhibition of
Matchbox and Lesney toys.

There are a great variety of attractions within reasonable driving distance of Chester, sufficient to cater for every taste. In Cheshire itself, there are working flour mills at Bunbury, near Tarporley, and at Stretton, in Farndon, as well as a Georgian cotton mill at Quarry Bank, Styal. There are numerous delightful villages and an impressive array of country houses from a number of centuries. The history of salt production, a traditional industry in Cheshire since Roman times, can be followed at the Salt Museum in Northwich, while the more scientifically inclined might prefer a visit to Jodrell Bank. Chester Zoo lies about two miles from Chester in 100 acres of landscaped grounds. One of the most beautiful zoos in the north of England, it has a Tropical House and an Aquarium, as well as a new Chimpanzee House, opened in 1989.

Westwards across the Dee lies Wales with its impressive mountain scenery and

TOP: *The huge dish of the world's largest steerable radiotelescope at Jodrell Bank Science Centre is a familiar sight. There is also a 'hands on' exhibition and a planetarium with* regular 'solar system flights'.

ABOVE: *Salt production is a major industry in Cheshire. Once mined from beds deep below the Cheshire Plain, it is* now pumped to the surface as brine. *The Salt Museum at Northwich provides a unique insight into the history and development of the industry.*

LEFT: *The village of Malpas was the birthplace of Bishop Heber, composer of many well-loved hymns. The 14th-century church of St Oswald is worth visiting for its magnificent bossed ceiling and Flemish window panels.*

ABOVE: *The Ellesmere Port Boat Museum lies at the end of the Chester Canal, where it joins the River Mersey. It boasts the largest floating collection of inland waterways craft.*

BELOW: *Chester Zoo has one of the largest wild cat collections in the country. This rare Siberian tiger cub is a testament to the success of the zoo's breeding programmes.*

breezy coastal resorts. Among the splendid castles to be seen here are those of Bodel-wyddan, Chirk and Conwy.

The Wirral Peninsula to the north is outstandingly beautiful and offers unri-valled sporting and recreational facilities. Parkgate is of interest because it was once an important ferry port serving Chester. The Port Sunlight Heritage Centre details the history of the village which was built in the 19th century by the industrialist Vis-count Leverhulme to house his workers.

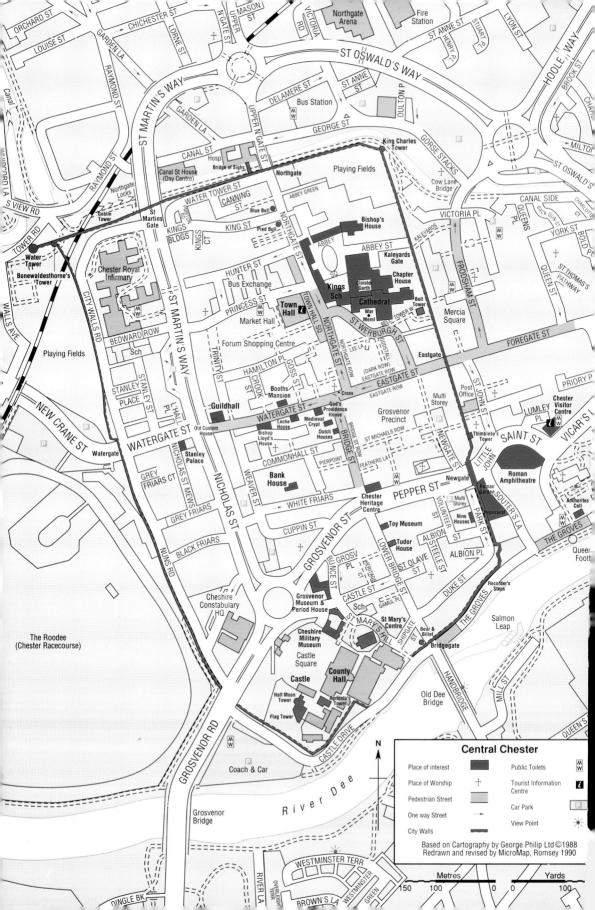

Central Chester

Place of interest	■
Place of worship	+
Pedestrian Street	
One way Street	
City Walls	
Public Toilets	MW
Tourist Information Centre	i
Car Park	P
View Point	✳

Based on Cartography by George Philip Ltd ©1988
Redrawn and revised by MicroMap, Romsey 1990

Metres 150 100 0 100
Yards

N